WITHDRAWN

Aromatic Teas and Herbal Infusions

Laura Fronty

PHOTOGRAPHS BY
Yves Duronsoy

CLARKSON POTTER/PUBLISHERS

NEW YORK

Published by Clarkson N. Potter/Publishers, 201 East 50th Street, New York, New York 10022. Member of the Crown Publishing Group.

Random House, Inc. New York, Toronto, London, Sydney, Auckland

http://www.randomhouse.com/

CLARKSON N. POTTER, POTTER, and colophon are trademarks of Clarkson N. Potter, Inc.

Originally published in French as *Tisanes et Infusions*, written by Laura Fronty and illustrated by Yves Duronsoy, © 1996 by Les Editions du Chêne-Hachette Livre. Translated from the original by L. M. Isaac.

Printed in Spain.

Library of Congress Cataloging-in-Publication Data is available upon request.

ISBN 0-517-70876-0

10 9 8 7 6 5 4 3 2 1

First American Edition

Contents

PREFACE

For years, herbal tea evoked the amber tones and gentle, honeylike perfume that emanated from my bath once I had immersed a sachet of leaves and flowers in the water. This lime-leaf bath was soothing and helped me to fall asleep. The bathtub took on all the richness of those beautiful yellow and green tints as I submerged myself in its warmth and then stepped out, slipped on an oversized bathrobe, and headed off to dreamland.

Of course, there was also chamomile tea, bitter as a punishment, which is generally administered to alleviate digestive problems or migraine headaches. Infusions made with vervain or delicately lemon-scented balm were savored on summer evenings on the terrace in Provence, and mint tea, hot and sweet yet so refreshing, was forever associated with the little copper teapots and the tiny, ornate glasses of Marrakesh cafés.

When I discovered Egypt, I came across an as yet unknown drink that was red and sweet like grenadine, with just a hint of acidity. Even its melodic name—*karkadé*—exudes the exotic and otherworldly flavor that is so evocative of life near Elephantine Island in Assouan.

And then there's the Lebanese white coffee, made by my friends Christine and Dina, which despite its name has absolutely nothing to do with coffee and captivates with its sublime orange blossom perfume.

And finally there was "everyday" tea, which has punctuated the day in the ritual that goes back to my early childhood: the round teapot, the darkish liquid with its cloudy veil of milk.

It is perhaps experiencing all these tastes and colors, coupled with a natural curiosity, that has always drawn me to the plants and flowers that have given life to a book dedicated to plants and to the hot, cold, or iced drinks made from them.

$\mathcal{I}$NTRODUCTION

Man and plants have been intertwined for many millennia. Long before the birth of agriculture, prehistoric man knew the healing virtues of certain wild plants and herbs.

This relationship is demonstrated by the discovery of the archeological remains of a man dating to more than six thousand years ago in Mesopotamia (present-day Iraq). This ancestor of the Neanderthal was found buried under a blanket of petals and leaves. Pollen analysis reveals that these leaves were medicinal plants, believed to be possessed

of multiple virtues. Most likely, the first men chewed the plants they gathered from their environment, adopting those that were beneficial and discarding the others. The invention of fire followed, permitting plants to be steeped in boiling water.

Besides Mesopotamia, Egypt was one of the great civilizations of antiquity to recognize the healing powers of plants. More than two thousand years before the common era, an Egyptian scribe wrote, "Here begins the book of remedies for all parts of the human body."

TISANES
INFUSIONS
HERBS TEAS
THÉS
TCHAÏ
DECOCCIÓNES
JARABE
VERVEINE · LIPPI
MINTH · MEN
TILLEUL · TÜ
MATRICAIR
CAMOMI
SALVI

■ The History of Tea: Born in China or in India?

The oldest and most renowned of all steeped plants is tea. Legend has it that in A.D. 2737, the emperor-god Chen-Nung was heating water under a tree when a gust of wind scattered leaves into the boiling liquid. The emperor drank this deliciously perfumed, amber-colored water and found it extraordinary. Chen-Nung went on to share the secret of this magic drink prepared with the leaves from the tea tree (*Camellia sinensis*), along with many other plant-based recipes. He is often credited with the invention of agriculture and botanical science, as well as the development of the basics of medicine, which he described in the *Pen Tsrao,* a catalog of hundreds of plants and their uses.

For Indians, however, tea was born in Bengal and the traditional story behind it is much less serene than that of Chen-Nung:

There was once a prince named Darma who, after years of debauchery, became a Buddhist monk. In order to expiate his previous sins, he made the vow never to sleep again. He resisted sleep for years and years—until one fateful day. When he awoke, he was so overwhelmed by guilt that he cut off his eyelids and buried them on the spot.

Years later, a monk came upon the exact place where this had happened and saw a mysterious shrub growing there. He took some of its leaves and placed them in boiling water. This brew would later become his only beverage. Upon leaving, he took some of the seeds

of this miraculous plant to sow around his home. Ever since that day, the Assam Hills have been covered with green tea shrubs and the "celestial drink" has become one of the ways through which man may return to his essence.

Whether from China (where it then spread to Japan) or India, tea is inseparable from the culture and philosophy in those parts of the world. It is also profoundly linked with Buddhism, as tea has always been considered essential to meditation.

■ The Ancient Art of Healing with Plants

Let's come back to medicinal herbs, which science has been refining for millennia and across many very different civilizations. As long ago

as 2,500 years before our time, the Hindus were using plants and spices to cure illness. According to the Vedic principles of medicine, it is vital to reinforce certain centers of energy (the chakras) in order to heal the body. Among the plants mentioned in the Veda, for example, are vervain and cloves, saffron and rose, coriander and fennel. Surprisingly, the Hindu Vedic texts describe plants and medical doctrines similar to those found in the writings of Hippocrates and Galen, two great sages of ancient Greece whose works are the precursors of modern Western medicine. These doctors prescribed bodily hygiene, bathing in thermal waters, and plant-based cures. These practices became very popular in the Greek gardens, especially as trade with

Africa and Asia permitted the import and cultivation of plants not found locally.

The ancient Egyptians also used plants in the arts of healing and beautifying. The Imhotep papyrus texts, which date from 2800 B.C., mention the use of mint, cardamom, cumin, fennel, marjoram, and juniper as medicinal and cosmetic ingredients, particularly as embalming oils.

A few centuries later, the commerce of medicinal herbs had become an extremely lucrative one for the Romans. In his book *Natural History,* Pliny (who was born in A.D. 23 and died when Vesuvius erupted in A.D. 79) writes at length of many different wild and cultivated plants used to treat symptoms and illnesses. His work, although sometimes a bit far-fetched scientifically, gives us a good idea of which plants were commonly used. Some of his recommendations remain valid to this day.

Pliny greatly appreciated mint, for it is "an odor that awakens the mind and a taste that stimulates the appetite," and "when taken in water, calms the gnawing feeling in the stomach." Cumin "diluted with water dissipates intestinal cramps and pain" and was believed to lighten the complexions of those who ingested it. Pliny also recommended anise infusions, which "taken in the morning with *Smyrnyum perforatum* and a bit of honey" eliminated bad breath.

MEDIEVAL MEDICINE

After the fall of the great Roman Empire, the Dark Ages submerged the Occident, and the economic and agricultural systems that stemmed from Roman civilization crumbled. Most of the aesthetic gardens in the Roman colonies went to seed, leaving only those used for nourishment, such as vegetable gardens and orchards. However, it was during the Dark Ages that the science of herbal medicine made great strides. Plants were consumed in various forms as infusions, powders, or essential oils obtained through the technique of steeping.

If the mainly Christian Occident had forgotten the charm of the purely aesthetic gardens so popular with Romans, the Greek and Roman scholars' ancient knowledge of plants survived through a sole and unique trustee: the Catholic Church.

This was the time when monks pioneered agriculture. Each monastery had its orchard, its vegetable garden, and a *hortus conclusus,* or closed garden. The closed garden was used to grow herbs that were both spiritual and curative. Lilies and roses, formerly woven into wreaths for Isis and Aphrodite by the Romans, were now used to worship the Madonna. These grew encircled by neat borders of balm, sage, rosemary, and simple marigolds. The monks spent long hours creating their marvelous herb gardens, painting and painstakingly describing each herb, its virtues as well as its side effects.

The importance of these gardens was such that around the year 800, the emperor Charlemagne sent each of his intendants a list of those plants to be cultivated in his empire. The document was known as *De Capitularis* or *De Vil-*

lis. Among the ninety plants listed, the iris and the rose came first and second, followed by cock mint or Tanacita, sage, rue, cumin, rosemary, anise, burdock, juniper, dill, savory, four different kinds of mint (pennyroyal, water, garden mint, and apple mint), marshmallow, mallow, coriander, and Clary sage.

These plants played important roles, both medicinal and culinary. They were often used in cooking, as they conferred taste and color to foods (color was an important element in the medieval culinary arts), and, perhaps most important, they preserved foods and masked the taste and odor of overaged meat.

In 1096, the Occident awoke from its long lethargy to the conquest of the mythical Orient and the first Crusades. Along the way to the East, crusaders came upon the Italian town of Salerno, which was the site of a renowned medical school founded by four doctors, an Arab, a Roman, a Greek, and a Jew, each of whom was the appointed guardian of the secular knowledge of their people. These men were recognized as true masters and their teachings would influence European medicine for centuries to come.

Upon returning from the Orient, the crusaders brought back a multitude of as-yet-unknown plants, seeds, and fruits. Among these was one plant that played a major role in the history of infusions: Sugarcane, or "honeyed reed" as it was first called, would later surpass honey as the most popular sweetener. But that is another story in itself.

POPULAR MEDICINE

Parallel to "official medicine," for which the rules and codes were made by the church and the ruling powers of the day, there was "popular medicine," an unofficial science that was handed down from one generation to the next. These recipes are often referred to as "old wives'" cures, which is in fact a poor translation from the original Latin term *bona fama,* meaning "good reputation."

In his *Book of Good Herbs,* Pierre Lieutaghi observes that "some enlightened sheepherders and peasants, who had been illuminated by the stars, gazing at the eyes of animals, the movement of water and the whispers of the universe, established their own reliable tradition, of which the last echoes come to us through the obscure writings of modern empiricists." These simple folk went about picking the wild plants of the woods and meadows and administered them to the ill. Their science was one acquired from years of coexisting with plants and from their deep love of nature.

THE DECLINE OF HERBS
AND INFUSIONS

The eighteenth century, with its enlightenment and reason, sought to purge medicine of its sometimes obscure and mystical practices.

Little by little, herbalists and their plants were forced into a sort of purgatory.

It was a situation that would not improve, and soon herbalists, as if they were some sort of modern sorcerers, became the objects of the ultimate anathema: They were forbidden to practice their profession. In France, a law promulgated by the Vichy regime simply eradicated the official diploma of "herbalist." To this day, French herbal prescriptions must be issued by a medical doctor and prepared by a pharmacist.

THE HERBAL
RENAISSANCE

Herbalists' shops are often seen in Spain, Germany, Holland, and Switzerland, and a multitude of aromas and perfumes emanate from the hundreds of jars of herbs, plants, and spices housed there.

At the same time, American supermarkets are beginning to carry herbal teas and infusions in sachets, and it is becoming easier to find various herbal blends that result in delicious, natural cocktails. On the menus of fine restaurants, it is becoming more and more fashionable to list after-dinner, house-blend herbal teas.

*T*ea harvest in northern India. Legend there attributes the birth of tea to an Indian disciple of Buddha.
FOLLOWING PAGES

THE ART OF TEAS AND HERBAL TEAS

The *Camellia sinensis* belongs to the greater family of camellias, originating in China and Japan. The narrow leaves of this shrub, which are bright, shiny green in color, are used for all sorts of teas.

In fact, there isn't just one tea, but many teas, all with different colors, flavors, and appearances. As with wine, teas have certain vintages, and their aromas differ greatly depending on the country or region of origin and the manner in which the leaves are gathered and cured.

Harvesting is done by hand. The extremity of the plant is the most important part, and the youngest leaves, along with two or three surrounding leaves, are delicately detached.

In Asia, the tea region has specific parameters, extending through China, Tibet, northern India, and Japan. Other countries cultivate tea, such as Kenya and, more surprisingly, the island of Madeira. In nineteenth-century America, an attempt was made to produce tea in South Carolina, and tea plantations similar to those used for cotton were

An envelope spills forth fragrant
tea leaves: an imaginative way
to convey a message—just
add the address and a stamp.
AT RIGHT

20

THE ART OF TEAS AND HERBAL TEAS

There are a thousand and one ways to appreciate this celestial
beverage: loose tea, bundles of medicinal tea, and a block
of tea bearing traditional designs in relief.

ABOVE

For centuries, the Chinese have practiced the art of
healing with plants or with teas, fragrant or otherwise.

AT LEFT

created. The exercise proved far too expensive, however, and was abandoned shortly thereafter.

CHINA, INDIA, AND CEYLON

Teas are generally classified by regions of origin, such as China, India, and Ceylon (present-day Sri Lanka). The most well known Chinese teas are the Keemun teas: black tea with a fine flavor that the Chinese say is similar to that of orchids. The Lapsang souchong teas come from Fujian and are characterized by a smoky, almost tarlike perfume. Oolong, a hybrid of green tea and black tea, comes from Formosa (Taiwan) and has an extremely delicate aroma; it is also used for jasmine-scented teas. The leaves of green teas are not fermented, as are those of black teas. The most well known of the green teas is gunpowder tea, so named because the first sailors who tasted it said it had the same effect as a gunshot. Green teas are also produced in China, Japan, and Taiwan.

The Darjeeling teas are undoubtedly the most popular Indian teas in the world. Like Assam teas, Darjeelings come from northern India. They are robust, with a dark amber color when prepared, and often need to be "cut" with a few drops of milk or lemon.

The Ceylon teas are also popular. Their flavor varies depending upon which hills they were grown on as well as the season in which they were harvested (either spring or autumn).

THE ASPECTS OF TEAS

Tea comes in myriad, often surprising incarnations, whether black, green, or even white, presented as leaves, powders, or pressed, in the form of bricks or nests.

Black teas are teas that have been fermented, and the leaves may be purchased whole, broken, or ground.

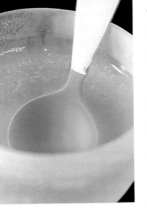

Green teas are cured using either steam or dry heat.

White tea is simply dried. Its name comes from the cinder-colored tint of its leaves.

In Japan, green tea leaves are first dried, then finely ground in a mill and purveyed in powder form.

In China, a tradition exists of pressed teas, which are shaped into a rolled nest, a rounded shingle, or a flat brick. These pressed teas are dark

Green tea served with delicious biscuits and tea-flavored jelly, beautifully presented for teatime at Mariage Frères in Paris.
PRECEDING PAGES AND AT LEFT

A finely wrought bowl makes the most of the tea's delicate aroma.
ABOVE

in color, and the top is stamped with a decorative pattern.

The Tibetans prefer tea in bricks, which they crumble into small pieces and boil with spiced rice and onions. Half-drink and half-food, this surprising tea is consumed with rancid yak butter.

AROMATIC AND PERFUMED TEAS

The tradition of perfumed teas started in the eighteenth century when certain British aristocrats began composing their own blends of tea. The most famous of these aromatic teas is undoubtedly the bergamot-scented Earl Grey variety. Charles, the Earl of Grey (1764–1845), who was prime minister under King William IV, learned of this delicious recipe from a Chinese mandarin. The tea was so well received that a London merchant asked the earl's permission to sell it. Earl Grey is composed of different sorts of teas, such as Keemun and Darjeeling.

Similar in taste to Earl Grey is Russian tea, which was the preferred blend of the Empress Elizabeth of Russia. It was undoubtedly introduced to Russia at the beginning of the eighteenth century by merchants traveling along the Silk Route to China.

Today aromatic teas are extremely popular and are made with many different ingredients, whether spices, fruit, or flowers. Among these are vanilla tea, black currant tea, apple tea (popular in Japan), hibiscus, mango, or rose tea—and the list goes on.

THE ART OF TEA

For the Japanese, the art of tea is one of ceremony and ritual, not just the simple preparation of a beverage. Without venturing too far into detail, we may glean a few elementary principles (which are also applicable to herbal teas) for making tea from the Japanese.

First, rinse the teapot with boiling water, so that it is hot. This will bring out all the tea's aroma.

Use about one teaspoon of tea per serving, plus one for the pot. If you're using high-quality tea, you should also use high-quality water. It should be pure and low in carbonates and other residues; spring water or mineral water is ideal.

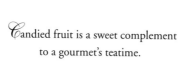

Candied fruit is a sweet complement to a gourmet's teatime.
AT RIGHT

The temperature of the water is also important: It should be simmering, not boiling.

Pour the water over the tea. Stir and let steep for two to six minutes, depending on the type of tea used and the tastes of your guests. Do not let the tea stand too long, as it will become bitter.

It is best to use separate teapots for teas and for herbal teas since traces of flavor may be left behind that might taint the flavor of the next brew. Purists even go so far as to use a different teapot for each type of tea.

■ Herbal Teas

The composition of herbal teas is extremely varied. Some are made of flowers—chamomile, lime, hibiscus; others of roots—licorice, rhubarb, angelica, mallow; fruits—bramble berries, juniper berries; seeds—coriander, cumin, fennel; rinds or barks—orange, lemon, willow, cinnamon; or even cornsilk.

These ingredients may be freshly cut or dried. Of course, you can dry your own ingredients, but you may also buy them in herb shops, specialized health food stores, and even supermarkets.

PLANTS FROM AFAR

Some plants used in herbal teas come from the other side of the world. One such example is star anise, for which China is practically the sole producer. Cinnamon comes from China or Sri Lanka. Nutmeg and its shell, mace, are cultivated in the Molucca Islands of Indonesia.

Hibiscus and karkadé come from Egypt, and vanilla comes from the areas near the Indian Ocean or Tahiti. Cardamom is produced in India and Cambodia. These spices are used to reinforce or soften the flavors of herbal teas, making them stronger or sweeter, depending on the tea.

A bit of advice: Don't hesitate to explore exotic grocery stores and Arab or African markets. These are the places where you can always find fresh mint, Vietnamese citronella, fresh or candied ginger, deliciously perfumed limes, as well as cardamom for massala tea, star anise, orange blossom water, or green tea.

FROM PLANTING
TO CONSERVATION:
THE HERB GARDEN

There is great satisfaction in planting, growing, and gathering one's own plants. It's the same feeling we get when we make homemade preserves and jams. Gazing upon carefully labeled jars or sachets instantly recalls images of hot summer days, of walking through fields in search of wild chamomile or aquatic mint.

We can dream about creating an herb garden in the image of those tended during the Middle Ages, where rosemary, thyme, lavender, boxwood, and vervain grew in perfectly ordered little rows and patches bordered by neatly trimmed geometric hedges. But it is not so very difficult to create your own aromatic herb garden for cooking and making infusions. Everything from chamomile, balm, and thyme to citronella, vervain, mint geranium, rosemary, and lavender may be homegrown. Most of these plants are easy to cultivate in almost any type of soil with a reasonable amount of

sunlight. As seeds, they should be sown during the month of May or, easier yet, bought as starters and replanted in the garden plot.

Those with green thumbs may want to play with cuttings, taken either from a friend's garden or from an unusual species found in the course of traveling. A cutting is taken in spring or autumn and stuck into a small pot filled with equal parts of potting compost and sand, which should be kept moist. The cutting usually takes root in about fifteen days. It can then be repotted in a larger container, where it will finish its growth before being transplanted in the garden.

*P*lants drying in the shadow of a trellis.
AT LEFT

The Jardin du Curé (parish priest's garden) at
Eugénie-les-Bains, in the Landes region of France.
The herbs and medicinal plants that grow here
are used daily to create healthful infusions.

ABOVE

Cuttings are the simplest way to expand an herb
garden. In cold weather, the plants are placed in a
makeshift greenhouse; here, an aquarium is covered
with a plate of glass, which is removed periodically
when condensation becomes heavy.

PAGE 36

Gathering Herbs

In the time of the Druids, there was a strict ceremony and time period for gathering certain plants. Priests, dressed in white linen robes, used golden scythes to cut the stems and branches of the plants.

Some dates in the Christian calendar had special significance. Saint Jean's Day, for example, was considered the ideal day for collecting medicinal plants. Without going so far as to specify exact dates and dress codes, every effort should be made to gather each plant at the best time of year.

Whether in the wild or in the garden, it is best to choose a sunny day for gathering—plants gathered on wet days tend not to dry as well and may mildew. Leaves, flowers, and fruits should be cut by hand, just after the morning dew has evaporated. Roots are best gathered in the evening. Flowers should always be picked when they first begin to bloom, and plants such as thyme, lavender, rosemary, and marjoram are best picked before they bloom, while the flowers are just buds, when the leaves contain maximum concentrations of aromatic essential oils.

Sometimes certain plants are hard to identify, or are totally unknown to us. It is advisable to purchase an illustrated botanical guide to avoid confusion. Those who especially enjoy botany can plant an herb garden specifically reserved for herbal teas and infusions, then identify each dried plant with its medicinal properties and even a few recipes.

Drying

After harvesting, spread your plants on a clean cloth, carefully eliminating any damaged parts. Roots should be cleaned with a quick rinse in running water and a light brushing to remove dirt. Leave the plants to dry in a well-ventilated place, away from light and moisture. Attics offer ideal conditions. Hanging plants from a wooden frame, a door, or a ceiling beam also works well.

The herb lover's pastime:
Labels indicate the name of each plant,
where it was gathered, and its properties.

ABOVE

Conserving

Once dried, the plants must be stored. Whatever the receptacle—jar, box, sachet, or paper bag—it is extremely important to use labels. Those who are orderly and precise will want to indicate the month of the harvest on the label. The ideal storage period for most plants is about one year, although some (roots in particular) will keep much longer. If you are storing your plants in glass jars, it it preferable to do so in a closed cupboard or closet, away from bright sunlight.

INFUSIONS, DECOCTIONS, AND MACERATIONS

Infusions

To make an infusion, leaves and flowers are left to steep in boiling water for several minutes. The quantity used is about one to two teaspoons of dried plants, or about a handful of fresh ones, for a half-quart of water. However, this quantity depends on personal taste and the plants used.

A kitchen or even a letter scale can be helpful in weighing with precision.

Decoctions

Roots, branches, stems, and peels as well as any other hard parts of the plants need to be prepared as decoctions in order to release and activate their beneficial principles.

To prepare a decoction, place the plants in a pot or pan of water and boil them for a certain length of time, depending on the nature of the plants. Times can range from a few minutes to an hour or so. Whatever the type of preparation, herbal teas should always be filtered before drinking.

Macerations

Some plants need to be soaked—in water, alcohol, wine, or oil—for several hours, or even days. The aromatic liquid is then filtered before being placed in a bottle and can generally be conserved for a long period of time.

*R*hubarb roots act as laxatives;
real licorice sticks are refreshing.
ABOVE

*S*lices of dried orange on a sprig of raffia,
mixed with laurel leaves.
AT RIGHT

The family herb cabinet with, *from left to right,* lime, chamomile, rhubarb roots, licorice, and peppermint—the essential ingredients for a good night's sleep and trouble-free digestion.

ABOVE

Sachets are tied up prettily and labeled before being shelved.

AT RIGHT

A slice of lemon and a piece of star anise impart a pleasant aroma and flavor to this digestive infusion.

PAGE 42

This method of preparation, maceration, is generally used for making liqueurs, elixirs, and plant- or fruit-based alcohols. Some require three weeks to a month of steeping prior to consumption.

TEAPOTS, HERBAL TEAPOTS, STRAINERS, AND OTHER ACCESSORIES

There is only one way to serve tea: with a teapot. Some tea drinkers, such as the Chinese and Japanese, prefer ceramic or cast-iron vessels. Others favor the eternal elegance of porcelain, especially antique pieces. Then there are those who wouldn't dream of doing without a silver or pewter teapot, with gently curving bellies rising up to meet a decorative lid with an ebony or ivory knob. Old teapots are often family heirlooms, passed down from generation to generation, and their insides may even bear traces of the teas enjoyed by ancestors. Beautiful, but not recommended for herbal teas, are metal teapots, particularly aluminum, which tend to impart a bad taste to herbs. Instead, use porcelain, glass, or earthenware pots for herbal teas.

For a long time, it was said that one should never wash a teapot, so as to let it become seasoned. Michael Smith, an English author and great tea connoisseur, takes strong exception to this notion. In *The Afternoon Tea Book*, Smith states that a too-thick coat of tannin in the pot will make the tea bitter and advises that the pot be washed carefully. To get rid of dark stains inside a teapot, place a few slices of lemon in boiling water, then pour the water into the teapot, and the tannin residue will dissolve.

This trick works with herbal teapots as well, especially those that have been used for particularly strong herbal teas such as licorice or mint.

Another indispensable tool for tea and herbal tea is the strainer, which can be replaced with a tea ball as long as it is large enough. It is absolutely vital that the plants are swished around in the hot water. Too-small tea balls or spoons compact the herbs and keep them from giving off their full aroma.

TEA IN BAGS OR SACHETS

Tea bags were invented in 1908 by a tea merchant named John Sullivan. The idea came to him when he decided to promote his teas by sending samples to his clients. He placed the samples in small, hand-sewn muslin "sachets," which he secured at the top with a bit of string. Mr. Sullivan's clients were of course smitten with his invention, which avoided the mess of tea leaves and saved them from having to wash their teapots.

Although the muslin sachet invented by John Sullivan was sufficiently large for the leaves to swell and infuse in the water, this is unfortunately not the case with most tea bags. The leaves are often ground into powder beforehand and are therefore depleted of flavor, which is, after all, one of the essential qualities of great teas or herbal teas.

A TOUCH OF SPICE, A HINT OF SWEETNESS

For many, herbal tea is synonymous with weak, lukewarm, and boring— or bitter, for those who have had the misfortune of coming up against an overpowering cup of chamomile tea! But infusions can be a source of relaxation and pleasure and a chance to discover new flavors and savors.

Never hesitate to blend different plants; for example, mint with licorice, apple and orange, or a little hibiscus for a rosy tint and a hint of tang. Using slices or zests of lemon will cut bitterness, and cinnamon, vanilla, star anise, cardamom, or mace all lend an exotic aura and a particular flavor to plants. Anyone can create personalized blends and aromas.

Unless you're dieting, there is absolutely no reason not to add a little honey or sugar to your herbal teas. Rock candy (crystallized sugar) is great for black teas; its taste is so pure

that it in no way changes the tea.

For herbal teas, white sugar, brown sugar, or honey are all delightful. For a special treat, add honey made from the same plant used for the tea—honey is made from thyme, lime, rosemary, orange, lavender, heather, and many other plants. Cane sugar, which you can buy as a liquid in bottles, is also an excellent and easy way to sweeten herbal teas.

A variety of sweet delights, from white
sugar, brown sugar, rock candy,
and sugar swizzle sticks to honey.
ABOVE AND AT RIGHT

HERBAL TEAS: THE CLASSICS

Chamomile, mint, lime, and vervain are probably the most well known and most widely appreciated infusion plants in the West.

Creative blending makes an excellent way to enjoy basic herbal teas. They may be consumed either hot or cold. Vervain and mint lend themselves particu-

larly well to chilled drinks, to which grapes, pieces of peach or melon, and other fruits may be added.

In the following pages, we will look at each of these popular infusion plants, explore history and virtues, discuss cultivation techniques, and learn the best ways to prepare and serve these grand classics.

Chamomile, which has a strong,
bittersweet apple taste,
makes a great digestive aid.
ABOVE AND AT RIGHT

■ Chamomile

IN THE GARDEN

Chamomile, which has a strong, bitter-sweet apple taste, makes a great digestive aid. There are two main varieties of chamomile tea. It is often difficult for the layperson to distinguish between these, although their differences are immediately obvious to the botanist.

The first type is German ("wild") chamomile, which proliferates in uncultivated fields, on slopes, and in many relatively nutrient-poor, rocky areas. Botanists call it *Matricaria recutita*. Its leaves are thin, veined, and slightly furry. The German chamomile flowers look like tiny daisies, with narrow white petals and a flat golden center.

The second type of chamomile is Roman ("harvest") chamomile. Though a cousin to the first variety, it does not belong to the same family. Its scientific name is *Anthemis nobile*. It is differentiated by its center, which is also gold but resembles a swollen cone, and is surrounded by white petals.

Roman chamomile is a very popular choice for herb gardens—it resembles a flower-covered lawn in summer. There are different varieties, with simple or double flowers, which are quite decorative. The seeds are sown in springtime in a fairly light soil. Chamomile likes sun or semishade. Chamomile flowers are best gathered in late summer or early autumn and then quickly dried.

IN THE TEAPOT

For herbal tea lovers, the two chamomiles possess practically the same characteristics. German chamomile is popular due to a "sour apple" aroma, from which it derives its nicknames. In Greek, it is called "apple from heaven," and in Spanish, *manzanilla* or "little apple." Its aroma is sweeter and less pronounced than that of Roman chamomile.

Prepared as infusions, chamomile is stimulating and beneficial for the stomach. It soothes digestive problems, calms the early stages of migraine headaches, and lessens low-grade fevers. Chamomile was used in the old French medicinal liqueur called *quinquina*.

To soften chamomile's distinctive bitter taste, honey is perfect (try acacia honey), as is sugar with half a vanilla bean split down the middle, or cinnamon (just a pinch in each cup).

IN THE BEAUTY CABINET

Blondes have long used German chamomile to emphasize the golden highlights in their hair: An infusion prepared with a generous handful of flowers per quart of water is used as a final rinse after shampooing.

A few handfuls of fresh or dried flowers—which may be tied up in a muslin sachet—tossed into baby's bath will calm the child and give the bathwater a pleasant fragrance.

Silvery lime leaves perfume June gardens, and its gentle infusion calms and induces sleep.

A detail of German chamomile,
resembling a miniature daisy.

ABOVE

A sculpture of a blackbird watches over a
bowl decorated with white chamomile blossoms,
a poetic nod to herbal infusion lovers.

AT RIGHT

■ Mint

IN THE GARDEN

Mint is even more complicated than chamomile—it has an amazing variety of colors, aspects, and even aromas. The basic odor of mint is fresh, piquant, and peppery, but can vary with each type of mint. All the varieties of mint belong to the same botanical family, *Labiatae,* and their lavender or rose-colored flowers blossom all summer long.

Spearmint, *Mentha virida,* also known as garden mint, balm mint, or Notre-Dame mint, is one of the most well known and commonly found varieties. Its narrow leaves are deep green and its flowers are grouped together in pointed "spearhead" formations. This is the mint used for Arabic mint teas.

Peppermint, *Mentha piperita,* also known as English mint or Mitcham mint, is immediately recognizable due to its peppery, piquant fragrance. This mint's leaves are wider than those of spearmint and the flowers are grouped in a rounder formation. This is the mint used for perfumes and by cosmetics manufacturers.

Mentha aquatica or water mint, as its name indicates, flourishes in moist environments. Its leaves are oval-shaped and sometimes downy. The aquatica flowers bloom in little round bouquets.

Pouliot mint, *Mentha pulegium,* dates to antiquity. In small balm or pennyroyal, it is easily identified by its thin, creeping stems, slightly rounded leaves, and tiny, rose-tinted flowers.

There are other, more unusual species that can be grown in the herb garden. For example, the decorative *panachée de creme* variegated mint (*M. suavolens 'variegata'*) or the *M. x gentilis 'variegata aurea'* are so called because of their striking gold-flecked leaves.

Before planting mint in an herb garden, know that mint does not like to be confined. In favorable conditions (good soil and semishade), mint plants will spread out in every direction, choking anything else that dares get in the way. Mint is sometimes better grown in containers.

IN THE TEAPOT

Spearmint and peppermint are highly appreciated for their digestive properties. As an infusion, mint stimulates gastric and bile secretions and is a great intestinal antiseptic. In olden days, some doctors claimed mint was an effective aphrodisiac.

Mint is lovely when blended with lime, its usual partner, but it also works marvelously with balm, green anise, vervain, orange blossom, and licorice.

•Mint and Cinnamon Infusion•

When the days become hot, this refreshing blend of cool mint and warm cinnamon hits the spot.

FOR EACH SERVING, USE:

½ HANDFUL FRESH OR DRIED MINT LEAVES

½ CINNAMON STICK

SUGAR (PREFERABLY CANE)

Pour boiling water over the mint and cinnamon. Let steep for 3 to 4 minutes, then add sugar.

•Mint and Licorice Infusion•

This blend may be enjoyed either hot or cold. You can combine any of a number of ingredients with spearmint: Try licorice, anise, fennel, or lemon. Licorice is sold as candy (licorice sticks), but for tea we use the real thing, crushed or broken into pieces. This infusion is both stimulating and good for digestion, but it is not recommended in large doses for those suffering from high blood pressure.

FOR EACH SERVING, COMBINE:

A FEW LEAVES OF SPEARMINT OR PEPPERMINT

A PINCH OF GROUND LICORICE

A PINCH OF ANISEED

A PINCH OF FENNEL

LEMON SLICES

Pour cold water over the plants and let steep for a few hours. You may also use boiling water, but the mixture should steep only for a few minutes. Filter, add a slice of lemon, and enjoy!

Delicious in summer, mint tea, with a hint of cinnamon, is refreshing and invigorating.
ABOVE LEFT

A literary companion: Peppermint and licorice make for an interesting match, to be enjoyed hot or cold.
AT RIGHT

•Mint Infusion for the Digestion•

For those who like special preparations, here's a great recipe:

FOR 1 LITER OF BOILING WATER, USE:

1½ TABLESPOONS AQUATIC MINT

1 TABLESPOON PEPPERMINT

2 TABLESPOONS ORANGE LEAVES

1½ TABLESPOONS GREEN ANISE

1½ TABLESPOONS VERVAIN

1½ TABLESPOONS LEMON BALM

2 GENEROUS TEASPOONS LIME LEAVES

2 SCANT TEASPOONS ORANGE BLOSSOM BUDS

Pour all the ingredients into a teapot or kettle and add boiling water. Let steep for a few minutes. This tea should be enjoyed after meals.

■ Household Remedies

THE SURPRISING VIRTUES OF PENNYROYAL

This variety of mint owes its name to *pulegium* (flea) in Latin. In ancient times, pennyroyal was believed to exterminate fleas and was sprinkled on floors, stuffed inside mattresses, and used in dogs' beds.

*P*reparing the elixir of mint and anise.
ABOVE

A siesta in the shade of a magnolia tree is the ideal time to savor a digestive infusion.
AT LEFT

•Mouth Rinse Elixir•

Mint has long been known to be a great breath freshener. Here is a recipe for an effective mouth rinse.

2 TEASPOONS MINT ESSENCE OR OIL

2 CUPS EAU-DE-VIE

1 TEASPOON GREEN ANISE

6 BLACK CLOVES

¼ CINNAMON STICK, CRUSHED

Pour the ingredients into a flask or shaker. Shake well and let steep for at least 48 hours.

Filter and place in a bottle. Mix a few drops in a glass of water for rinsing; do not swallow.

■ Lime

IN THE GARDEN

The decorative, silver-leafed lime tree often grows in cities and gardens, but, unfortunately, most lime trees possess no herbal benefits. The only variety that does is the unique (and most gorgeous of all) *Tilla cordata,* or common lime. Often reaching heights of more than thirty feet, its heart-shaped leaves and abundant flowers give off the delicious fragrance of lime in early June.

June is the right time to pick the flowers, just as they begin to open, and to dry them in the shade on a clean cloth. Once dry, lime retains its bright green-yellow color, as long as it is well protected from sunlight or overly bright artificial light.

IN FRONT OF THE MIRROR

Lime infusion may be used as a floral water that softens and soothes irritated skin and that also imparts a lingering, delicate scent.

IN THE TEAPOT

Lime is the most gentle of remedies. Taken as an infusion, lime is a total relaxant, psychologically as well as physically. Often, lime is combined with mint, vervain, or lemon balm, which gives its gentle flavor a hint of spice.

Although lime infusions are great for soothing jangled nerves, the beverages must be cooled before being drunk luke-warm: If consumed too hot, the infusion has the reverse effect.

Lime is also a great additive for bathwater, and is particularly effective in calming overexcited children. The leaves should be placed in a large cotton handkerchief (or other airy fabric) in order to allow the release of their soothing essence.

*A*fter drying, aromatic lime blossoms
are best preserved in a sealed jar.
AT LEFT

*T*he fragrant realm of Christine and
Michel Guérard. Behind the monastery walls
at Eugénie-les-Bains, France, vervain bushes
flourish in the Jardin du Curé.
FOLLOWING PAGE

■ Vervain

IN THE GARDEN

Odiferous vervain, *Lippia citriodora,* is aptly named; indeed, its powerful, lemony aroma pervades the plant's vicinity. Originally from Chile, this exotic version is a distant relative of *Verbena officinalis,* which is virtually odorless and a quite modest plant in general.

The leaves of the odiferous variety of vervain are narrow, light green, and rough in texture. This small, bushy tree is subtropical and cannot withstand cold climates. It thrives only in warm, sunny conditions. Given the right environment, it can grow to just over three feet tall and may be pruned like any other shrub.

In some gardens, vervain serves as a hedge surrounding the aromatic herb garden, adding its own fresh, lemony smell to the symphony of other herbal perfumes. The flowers, which are grouped into long "ears," come out at the end of May and are of no real interest to the gardener. In fact, it's better to remove them, so as to divert the plant's precious energy elsewhere.

In regions subject to winter freezes, vervain can be grown in pots and taken inside from October until around May. Vervain must be exposed to sunlight in order to produce highly perfumed leaves. Vervain is easily propagated from stem cuts, taken in spring, when it starts growing again.

The leaves are gathered throughout the summer, particularly once the bushes begin to blossom, generally in June.

In the teapot

Vervain is prepared as an infusion using fresh or dried leaves. It possesses slightly sedative virtues and soothes digestive discomfort. The infusion is generally taken just after meals. It is quite nice blended with mint, citronella, and other "digestive" plants such as fennel or green anise.

Be careful not to overdo it with vervain, as its active ingredients can irritate the stomach lining if taken in high doses over long periods of time.

• Blended Vervain Infusion •

Mix equal proportions of lime, balm, orange blossoms, green anise, and mint with 1½ tablespoons of vervain. Let steep for 5 minutes in a quart of boiling water and enjoy after a meal.

• Michel Guérard's Digestive Tea •

To make the blend, you will need:

4 tablespoons green anise

4 tablespoons fennel

4½ tablespoons citronella

2½ tablespoons vervain

Use about 3 tablespoons of this blend per serving. Let steep for 5 minutes in boiling water and consume after a meal.

Vervain infusions are always delicious hot or cold, especially when savored with fruit pastries.

AT LEFT

IN THE KITCHEN

Some cooks use vervain when cooking to impart a delicious aroma to white meat, particularly chicken. This is best done by placing the meat on a bed of vervain leaves and water and steaming it. Vervain is also a good substitute for citronella. Many Chinese recipes call for citronella, so if you have none on hand, a few leaves of vervain will do the trick nicely.

Vervain also makes a marvelous complement to ice cream: Pour a small quantity of a concentrated infusion over vanilla ice cream and enjoy the unique aroma.

Fresh, finely minced vervain leaves add an unusual touch to fruit salads with melon, mango, strawberry, or orange.

IN THE HOME

Vervain has a delicious aroma, even when dried. It is often used in the composition of potpourri. Here is a recipe for a potpourri combining all the colors and aromas of the garden of the Hesperides.

A beautiful potpourri of vervain, spices, and aromatic herbs.

ABOVE

A basketful of drying plants fills the kitchen with pleasant aromas.

AT LEFT

• Lemony Potpourri •

1⅔ CUPS VERVAIN LEAVES

¾ CUP SPEARMINT

3 TABLESPOONS ROSE-SCENTED GERANIUM

3 TEASPOONS LEMON THYME

3 TEASPOONS VERVAIN CITRONELLA

1 LIME ZEST

1 ORANGE ZEST

1 ZEST OF ½ GRAPEFRUIT

2 TABLESPOONS IRIS POWDER

3 TABLESPOONS MARIGOLD PETALS

A FEW DROPS OF ORANGE ESSENCE

First, mince all the leaves and zests and put them in a decorative bowl. Add the orange essence and sprinkle the marigold petals on top.

RECIPES FROM NEAR AND FAR

The term *infusion* covers many different preparations and drinks. Some are made with a water base, others with milk or alcohol. The plants, herbs, or spices are then steeped in these liquid bases.

The world is absolutely overflowing with sensations: heat, freshness, sunshine, spices, flowers . . . whether it be Arabic mint tea, Egyptian karkadé, Leb-

anese white coffee, Yemenite cardamom coffee, Argentinian maté, or Spanish cinnamon-chocolate, the exotic world of aroma beckons!

The liqueurs and elixirs cherished in the Old World are easily made, using special ingredients and methods of preparation. These beverages are delicious when served cold as aperitifs or as after-dinner drinks.

Colette's celebrated orange wine, served ice-cold as an aperitif. Tangy citrus notes of orange and lemon are softened by long weeks of maceration with vanilla beans.

AT RIGHT

■ White Coffee

The first time I heard of white coffee was at the end of a meal served by a Lebanese friend. I fully expected to discover some rare, unknown form of coffee, but instead out of the kitchen came little blown-glass cups brimming with a hot, transparent, and very sweet liquid that saturated the room with the exquisite aroma of orange blossoms.

The herbal tea known as white coffee is made with orange blossom water. Traditionally served after Lebanese meals, it is often accompanied by candied rose petals, served in tiny, delicate dishes.

White coffee, a marvelous sedative, calms the nerves and stimulates digestion after a particularly rich or heavy meal.

In Lebanon, orange blossom water is given to fussy babies; it is also used as perfume, either in the bathwater or directly on the skin.

•Dina's White Coffee•

YOU WILL NEED (PER SERVING):

1 TEASPOON ORANGE BLOSSOM WATER

1 LEMON ZEST

A FEW SUGAR CUBES

Paradoxically, Lebanese white coffee contains absolutely no coffee. Instead, it imparts the fragrance of an orange tree in bloom—an Oriental pleasure that is not to be missed.

AT LEFT

Cardamom coffee is prepared using Turkish blend and grated cardamom. Its aroma is powerful and exotic; green cardamom is the most fragrant variety.

PAGE 71

Heat the water in a pan. When it starts to simmer, add the orange blossom water and the lemon zest. As soon as the mixture boils, remove it from the heat.

Serve very hot and very sweet, preferably in tiny, decorative Lebanese-style glasses. To avoid breaking the glasses with the boiling-hot tea, place a little spoon in each glass before pouring.

■ Happy Arabia Coffee

Coffee was born in Yemen, on the high plateaus, a region that used to be called "Happy Arabia." According to legend, a young shepherd was tending his goats one day when he noticed they were acting quite strangely, almost as if they were drunk. He realized that the goats had eaten the red berries from a nearby shrub.

The young shepherd then ate some of the berries himself, became quite agitated, and found that he could not fall sleep for hours afterward. He told his story to the Imam of his village, the wise Sufi.

The old Imam also ate the berries but found them nasty in their raw form. He decided to crush them and cook them in water. The resulting beverage was just as unpalatable, so he tried cooking them in the embers of the campfire, as was done with certain grains. He then ground up the now-black berries and cooked them in water. The drink was so bitter that he had to add a generous amount of honey to sweeten it. Then the miracle happened: the Imam's mind became clear and sharp, and instead of nodding off to sleep as usual, he remained in a heightened state of awareness all night long. He was so excited by his discovery that he gave the drink to all of his companions that they, too, might enjoy its powers during long nights of prayer.

This story's religious and traditional content closely parallels that of tea, which pertains to the meditations of the Buddhists.

Coffea arabica, the shrub that produced the amazing beans, originally came from Kaffa, and the drink carried the same name. It later became known as *kawa,* which signifies "that which excites, which gives wings," and also refers to a famous Persian ruler who flew straight to the heavens, powered only by the wings of his mind.

• Liwan's Cardamom Coffee •

This coffee drink in no way resembles what we generally think of as coffee. In Lebanon, a *kawa helwé* (sugared coffee) is ordered, unless of course you prefer it *seda* (without sugar) or *wassat* (neither too sweet nor too bitter).

This delicious coffee may also be found at Liwan's, a warm and welcoming Parisian shop that carries Lebanese clothes, house linens, and other items for the home.

The cardamom is ground with its hull along with the coffee beans. You need about five hulls per two pounds of coffee.

FOR EACH CUP OF WATER, YOU WILL NEED:

½ TEASPOON SUGAR

1 ½ TEASPOONS CARDAMOM-COFFEE BLEND

Boil the water for 1 minute. Add the sugar, stir, and boil again. Add the coffee and let it heat until simmering, making sure it doesn't boil over or for too long.

Of course, the ideal is to use a little metal coffeepot with an extra-long handle, called a *rakwé,* which can be put directly on the burner.

•Lemonade•

Here is a really old recipe for lemonade, found in a book dating from the end of the last century. The only change I made is to reduce the amount of sugar by half.

FOR 1 QUART, YOU WILL NEED:

⅔ CUP GRANULATED SUGAR

3 CUPS WATER

2 LEMONS, JUICY AND UNTREATED

Pour the sugar and water into a pot and stir until the sugar has dissolved. Wash the lemons and remove the peels, being careful to leave the bitter white pulp on the lemon. Cut up the lemon peel and let it marinate in the sugarwater.

Squeeze the lemons and remove any seeds. Mix and let stand for 4 to 5 hours.

Filter the mixture and pour into a carafe. Add lots of ice and serve very cold. You may also add carbonated water to this drink.

•Hot Lemon•

With the advent of cold weather and wintertime colds, a mixture of hot lemon and honey is ideal for soothing sore throats and may be consumed as desired.

PER SERVING, YOU WILL NEED:

1 LEMON

1 CUP HOT WATER

2 TEASPOONS ORANGE- OR

LAVENDER-BLOSSOM HONEY

Squeeze the lemon into the hot water and stir in the honey.

This tangy golden fruit of legend, which Hercules discovered in the garden of Hesperides near Gibraltar, is often served with tea and other herbal infusions. Served cold, lemonade is one of the simple pleasures of summer.

AT RIGHT

■ Egyptian Karkadé

Oddly enough, this drink prepared from the scarlet flowers of the hibiscus (*Hibiscus sabdifera*) is known only in the region surrounding the Nile River. Karkadé resembles a sort of grenadine infusion, especially in its deep red color. However, its taste is much closer to that of lemonade—very tangy.

Karkadé is extremely rich in vitamin C and may be consumed hot or cold. In Egypt, it is served in all the cafés and is invested with the same traditional importance as Moroccan mint tea. Like mint tea, karkadé is prepared with generous amounts of sugar and enjoyed after (or between) meals.

To make karkadé tea, buy some of the dried hibiscus flowers, which are blackish-red in color, that are sold in an Egyptian marketplace (the *souk*). You can find hibiscus flowers in herb specialty shops as well as in grocery stores that sell products from all over the world.

•Assouan-Style Karkadé•

In the town of Assouan, on the banks of the Nile, karkadé is served ice cold, to better refresh the desert dwellers' sand-parched throats.

Use a heaping teaspoon of dried hibiscus flowers per serving. Pour boiling water over the flowers and let the mixture steep for at least an hour. The longer it steeps, the more its acid flavor dissipates and its ruby-red color intensifies. Add sugar to tone down the acidity.

In Egypt, the ruby-colored karkadé is enjoyed steaming hot or ice cold and very sweet, like mint tea.

ABOVE

To make an apple infusion, all you need is some dried apple peel. As strange as it may seem, they make a truly delicious taste, closely resembling that of rum—but without the alcohol. Pour boiling water over the minced apple peel and let steep for about ten minutes. Sweeten to taste and enjoy it nice and hot. You can also dry some apple slices, which you then cut into smaller pieces and add to a hibiscus infusion.

FOLLOWING PAGES

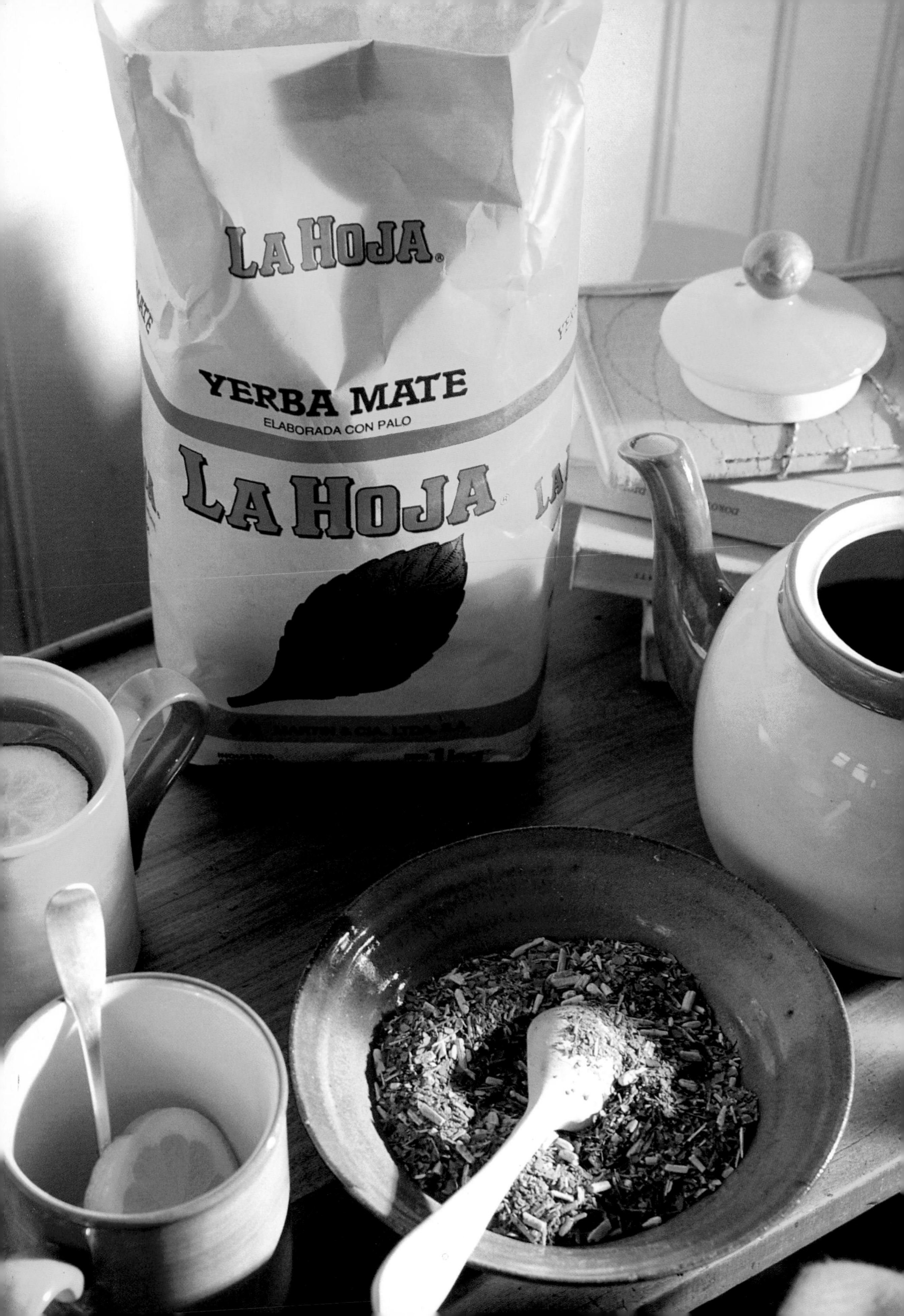
LA HOJA
YERBA MATE
ELABORADA CON PALO
LA HOJA

■ Maté or Argentinian Tea

Maté is a very popular drink in Argentina, where it generally replaces normal tea. This traditional beverage comes from the Indians of Argentina, Brazil, and Paraguay, countries where the *Ilex paraguariensis* grows. A sort of local holly plant, its leaves are ground to make this special tea.

When the Jesuit missionaries arrived in the area to convert the Indians to Christianity, they themselves were converted to faithful consumers of this drink, which was baptized "Jesuits' tea."

Because the leaves contain caffeine, this tea is a fairly strong stimulant. Avoid letting the leaves steep for too long, as the maté will become bitter. You may want to add a slice of lemon or orange.

Maté is prepared just like tea, using about a teaspoon of leaves per serving. Pour boiling water over the tea and let steep for 3 to 4 minutes.

• Infusion for the Office •

If you need a pick-me-up when the day is getting a little long, try this tea instead of regular tea, especially if you tend to suffer from insomnia.

You can also add hibiscus flowers, apple, orange peel, or vanilla to the following basic recipe. To add zest to this gentle tea, cinnamon or ground ginger may be substituted for the vanilla.

PEEL FROM ½ APPLE OR A FEW CUBES
OF DRIED APPLE
A ZEST OF ORGANIC ORANGE
4 TEASPOONS HIBISCUS FLOWERS
2 CUPS WATER

Finely dice the apple peel and orange zest. Heat the teapot in advance and add the hibiscus, apple peel, and orange zest. Add boiling water and let steep for at least 10 minutes. Sweeten to taste.

■ Aromatic Teas

These traditional exotic teas are reminiscent of *A Thousand and One Nights,* mingling the heavenly aromas of flowers and spices.

INDIAN TEA OR CHAI

In India, tea in no way resembles what we have come to know as tea. Prepared with Darjeeling or another tea of Indian origin, it is mixed with several different kinds of spices. This mixture of spices, called *massala,* contains green cardamom, ginger, cinnamon, and sometimes pepper and other spices.

Boiled milk is substituted for water. Sweetened condensed milk diluted with water is often used, as chai is supposed to be very sweet.

In winter, when the days are cold and gray, this typical Indian-style tea is a wonderful pick-me-up.

MINT TEA

Mint tea is a traditional drink in North Africa and the Middle East, and is always served to welcome friends, family, or visitors from afar.

It is prepared using green tea—also known as gunpowder tea—and a bouquet of fresh spearmint, called *nâa-naa* in Morocco. In his book *The Taste of Morocco,* Robert Carrier notes that mint tea is used to "cure insomnia, calm the nerves, sharpen the senses and wake up those who are drowsing."

•Moroccan Mint Tea•

Mint tea is served very sweet and hot, ideally in little traditional tea glasses decorated with gold, multicolored arabesques.

Place 2 or 3 teaspoons of green tea into a metal teapot (copper or silver) that can be placed directly over the heat.

Pour a small amount of boiling water over the tea and allow the leaves to absorb and swell. Next, fill the teapot with hot water and place it on the burner for 1 to 2 minutes. Then remove the teapot from the heat and add a small handful of spearmint leaves. Place the teapot on the burner again for 1 more minute. Add sugar (about one and a half cubes per serving).

Serve very hot in small glasses.

•Rose, Orange, and Cinnamon Tea•

This is a delightfully scented tea, a mix of pungent rosebuds with orange zest and cinnamon that may be prepared hot or iced. The blend also makes a fragrant winter potpourri. This tea is best without milk, with just a slice of lemon or orange.

FOR EACH SERVING, YOU WILL NEED:

1½ TEASPOONS DARJEELING OR CEYLON TEA

A FEW CRUSHED ROSEBUDS

ZEST OF ½ ORANGE, FINELY MINCED

1 PINCH GROUND CINNAMON

OR A FEW SMALL PIECES

Mix the tea, rosebuds, orange zest, and cinnamon and prepare the tea as usual.

A steaming hot cup of massala tea, sweetened with pieces of candied ginger.

PER SERVING, YOU WILL NEED:

ABOUT 1 TEASPOON PER SERVING DARJEELING

OR CEYLON TEA

1 PINCH CARDAMOM

1 PINCH GINGER

1 PINCH CINNAMON

1 PINCH POWDERED VANILLA

BOILED MILK

1 TEASPOON GRANULATED SUGAR

•Réunion Island Massala Tea•

Located in the Indian Ocean, Réunion Island has a highly diverse population that includes descendants of the Bretons, Chinese, and the proud Malabars from the southernmost reaches of India. These Indians brought both their religion and their customs to the island, including massala tea, which should be enjoyed in the shade of the *varangue* (veranda). Massala is made by combining hot spices with the soft taste of vanilla beans from sweet orchids—the pride and joy of many a plantation on the surrounding islands, including Saint Anne, Saint André, and Bras-Panon.

Warm the teapot beforehand by rinsing it with boiling water, then add the tea and spices. Fill teapot with milk and sweeten. Serve very hot.

•Vanilla Tea•

This is a gently perfumed classic tea. It can be store-bought in ready-to-serve sachets. However, you may prefer to prepare it yourself with fresh ingredients.

FOR EACH SERVING, YOU WILL NEED:

1½ TEASPOONS CEYLON TEA

1 VANILLA BEAN, DICED

Prepare the tea as usual and add the vanilla, which will steep along with the tea, slowly imparting a gentle aroma.

Vanilla—whole or powdered—cinnamon, and green cardamom are essential ingredients of Indian chai tea.

ABOVE

The lustrous, dark vanilla bean harbors all the fragrant subtlety of the tropics.

AT RIGHT

'Portrait of Space', Near Siwa, 1937.
Magritte saw this photograph in
London in 1938 and it is thought to
have inspired his painting *Le Baiser*.
(Lee Miller)

■ Alcohol-Based Macerations and Infusions

•Marie's Tarragon-ade•

This is an old recipe given to my grandmother by her friend Marie. It is easy to make and even better when you use homegrown tarragon fresh from the garden. It makes an excellent after-dinner drink.

In antiquity, tarragon was believed to be useful for treating venomous bites, particularly dragon bites, which eventually gave rise to the popular name for tarragon, "dragon grass."

You will need:

1 big handful of fresh tarragon

(about ⅓ cup)

1 vanilla bean, halved down the middle

1 quart of 45-proof alcohol or brandy

5 cups sugar

1 quart water

Place the tarragon leaves and bean in a jar or bottle. Pour the alcohol over them and allow to stand for 3 or 4 days. Make a syrup using the sugar and water and add it to the mixture. Let steep for another 15 days and then filter.

Pour into a bottle or decanter and add a branch of tarragon, just to make it look decorative. This liqueur is an excellent after-dinner drink.

•Creme de Menthe•

This recipe comes from a book by Suzanne Fonteneau, *Syrups, Liqueurs, Household Drinks.* It is full of surprising, often long-forgotten drink recipes that are great fun to rediscover. Her creme de menthe is really easy to make. Contrary to its name, this liqueur contains absolutely no cream, nor does it have a creamy texture. The term *creme* was once used to designate certain plant-based alcoholic beverages.

You will need:

1½ cups spearmint

1 teaspoon aniseed, crushed

1 teaspoon coriander seeds, crushed

1 quart of 45-proof alcohol

4½ cups sugar

3 cups water

First, marinate the mint leaves and seeds in the alcohol for 8 days. Then make a syrup from the sugar and water. Filter the mint mixture and add the syrup to it. Pour into a nice decanter or bottle.

•Colette's Orange Wine•

In her 1932 book *Prisons and Paradise,* the French author Colette shared her recipe for orange wine:

"A double flask, in old crystal, contains 'orange wine' that is at least five years old.… It was made one year when the oranges from the Hyères region were particularly gorgeous and deep, ripe red. Into four liters [quarts] of dry,

yellow Cavalaire wine, I poured a liter of fine armagnac only to hear my friends exclaim: 'What a waste! Such a fine *eau-de-vie*! Sacrificing it to an undrinkable ratafia!' Among these cries of protest, I sliced four oranges and a lemon, which a few minutes earlier swung peacefully on its branch, a vanilla bean, silver as an old man's hair, and 600 grs. [3 cups] of cane sugar and drowned them in the alcohol. A pot-bellied jar closed with a cork top and a cloth took care of the marination, and 50 days later, all that was left for me to do was to filter and bottle it."

•Hangman's Liqueur•

The hangman is the orange, which is suspended over a jar filled with alcohol. There are several versions of this recipe, which tastes a bit like curaçao.

Most important is to make sure that the orange never comes in contact with the alcohol. One way of doing this is to "thread" the orange (draw a string through it with a big needle) and then attach the string around the neck of the jar containing the alcohol. You then close the jar tightly—with a lid if possible, and if not, due to the string, with plastic wrap.

YOU WILL NEED:

1 QUART EAU-DE-VIE OR 45-PROOF ALCOHOL

1¼ CUPS SUGAR

1 UNPEELED ORANGE

After pouring the alcohol and the sugar into the jar, hang the orange above the liquid. Close the jar hermetically and store it in a dark place for 2 months. When the orange has hardened completely, throw it out, filter the alcohol, and pour into a decanter.

•Parfait Amour•

The name alone says it all! This recipe for a thyme-based liqueur was also borrowed from Suzanne Fonteneau's book.

YOU WILL NEED:

⅓ CUP LEMON ZEST

3 TABLESPOONS THYME

2 TABLESPOONS CINNAMON

1 TABLESPOON NUTMEG

1 TABLESPOON CORIANDER SEEDS

2 CLOVES

1 VANILLA BEAN

1 CUP BRANDY OR 45-PROOF ALCOHOL

7½ CUPS SUGAR

½ CUP WATER

Marinate the lemon zest and seasonings in the alcohol for 1 week. Make a syrup of the sugar and water and mix the ingredients together. This second mixture should stand for another week. Filter, then pour into a decanter or a pretty bottle.

Just a "finger of orange wine," in an old tumbler that had lost its handle, as described by Colette.
AT LEFT

FLORAL RATAFIA LIQUEURS

Orange blossoms, carnations, roses, and violets are all classic favorites for "old ladies' liqueurs." Floral alcohols were called ratafias, an old Creole word designating rum-marinated preparations made with flowers, leaves, fruits, and berries.

•Carnation Ratafia•

Cloves contain an essence that is often used by perfume manufacturers as an imitation carnation aroma. Steeping the cloves in alcohol enhances the aroma of carnations in this drink.

YOU WILL NEED:

3½ CUPS OF SWEET PINK CARNATION PETALS

2 TABLESPOONS CLOVES

2 TABLESPOONS CINNAMON

3 QUARTS BRANDY, 45-PROOF ALCOHOL,

OR LIGHT RUM

4 CUPS SUGAR

2 CUPS WATER

Separate the carnation petals and throw away the white part (the unguis) at the base of the petals. Let petals and spices marinate in the alcohol for 2 months. Once the mixture is done steeping, prepare a syrup with the sugar and water and blend the two together. Mix well and pour into a pretty decanter.

•Vespetro•

This old "household liqueur," as homemade drinks used to be called in Europe, probably came from Italy. Reputed to help difficult digestions, this recipe is adapted from a text found in *Le Pot au Feu,* a cookbook from 1909.

TO PREPARE 1½ QUARTS OF LIQUEUR, THERE ARE TWO DIFFERENT VERSIONS. YOU WILL NEED EITHER:

2 TEASPOONS CORIANDER

2 TEASPOONS ANGELICA

2 TEASPOONS CARAWAY

2 TEASPOONS FENNEL

1 QUART BRANDY

3 CUPS SUGAR

⅔ CUP PURE WATER

OR:

2 TEASPOONS CORIANDER

2 TEASPOONS ANGELICA

1 TABLESPOON ANISEED

1 QUART BRANDY

3 CUPS SUGAR

⅔ CUP PURE WATER

Crush all the seeds in a mortar, stopping short of grinding them into a powder. The mortar can be replaced by a coffee grinder, if you are careful to crush and not pulverize. Place the grains in a jar, then add the alcohol. Allow to marinate for 15 days, preferably in the sun, stirring from time to time. Filter the brew. Prepare a syrup with the sugar and water and add an equal quantity to the brew. Place in a hermetically sealed bottle or decanter.

To achieve a pure liquid when filtering liqueurs and infusions, place a cotton pad at the bottom of the funnel.

PLANTS AND WELL-BEING

Some plants have been known since time immemorial for having medicinal virtues. It's really quite simple to create a plant-based medicine cabinet at home to have remedies on hand in the event of small injuries or not-too-serious illnesses.

In olden days, the mistress of the house often used heather or cornsilk to speed up sluggish intestinal activity and dandelion or dog's tooth for a "spring-cleaning" of the body. Violets were picked in March and their petals stored

for autumn and winter colds. Women ventured into summer fields to pick cornflowers used in lotions to soothe tired eyes and red poppies to cure insomnia. In their back gardens, they grew everything they needed for the beauty of their hair and skin, from lilies and marigolds to roses and sage. Hawthorn was gathered along country paths and used to calm the nerves, and fresh burdock was picked to remedy insect bites: The leaves were rubbed on the bite to kill the pain and reduce inflammation.

An autumn infusion: Fragrant steam envelops a cluster of mauve heather.

ABOVE

Pansies, heather, cardamom, star anise, and cornflower: a palette of colors
and scents for creating infusions or simply to drink with the eyes.

AT RIGHT

■ Hawthorn

There is no doubt that Marcel Proust remains unsurpassed when it comes to describing the fleeting, springtime splendor of the white hawthorn with its seemingly snow-covered hedges:

"I had to run to catch up with my father and grandfather who were calling me; they were surprised that I hadn't followed them along the path that rose towards the fields. The air was impregnated with the smell of hawthorn. The hedge somehow made me think of a chain of chapels that disappeared under the swath of blossoms amassed into what resembled altars: above them, the sun shone down to form a luminous patch, as if it had come through a skylight. The scent of hawthorn spread out like some kind of unctuous physical presence, and I felt like I could almost be standing before the Virgin Mary—each flower a little version, carrying its bouquet of stigmas, tiny and shining little veins, as flamboyant as those openwork ornaments in the rood screen or the transoms of the stained glass windows and which surged forth in the white flesh of strawberry blossoms."

Hawthorn flowers or buds must be picked quickly, and immediately dried on a cloth in the shade.

Hawthorn infusion, with its gentle, honeyed savor, is highly reputed for calming and relaxing stressed nerves. The recommended dose is 1 tablespoon per cup of boiling water. Hawthorn flowers can be blended with lime, sweet woodruff, balm, or passion flowers as well as with orange blossom water.

■ Cornflower

In French popular tradition, cornflowers picked at summer harvest time were called *casse-lunettes* ("spectacles breakers") and were reputed to improve the sight of blue eyes.

To help ease the fatigue of sensitive eyes (whatever color they may be!), a wash made with cornflower infusion works wonders. Use about ¼ cup of flowers for 1 quart of boiling water. Let it steep for about 10 minutes and, once cooled, use it as an eyewash.

Cornflower is also a diuretic: The infusion, prepared as above, helps alleviate the retention of excess fluids.

Cornflower petals, although odorless, give a beautiful touch of color to potpourri. They are also used to pep up the colors of certain perfumed blends of tea, such as violet tea.

■ Heather

Although considered a symbol of autumn, heather, with its lavender and pink flowers, actually starts blooming in July. You can find it blooming for months on end in forests and uncultivated moors, often near big, wavy ferns.

Heather tea is a strong diuretic and is often prescribed in cases of urinary infections. It is sometimes used in conjunction with cornsilk and cowberries.

This infusion should be prepared using ¼ cup of heather flowers for 1 quart boiling water.

As this tea doesn't have a pronounced flavor, you may want to add some heather honey.

■ Cherries

Wild cherries, Bing cherries, morello cherries —there are numerous varieties of fruits in this family, of various shades and sizes. For teas, the stems are used to make diuretic infusions. The stems must be prepared by decoction: Boil ⅓ cup of stems in 1 quart of water for about 10 minutes.

Cherry stems can be prepared with cornsilk, olive-tree leaves, or apple peel to give this somewhat weak infusion a nicer flavor.

■ Lemon

The golden fruit from the garden of the Hesperides possesses only virtues! The crusaders brought lemons to Europe when they returned from the Mediterranean regions, where lemons had been cultivated since antiquity. Rich in vitamin C, lemons have always been loaded into the holds of ships setting sail for distant lands to reduce the sailors' risk of getting scurvy from a lack of fresh fruit.

The essence extracted from lemon zest is a powerful antiseptic. In winter, when you have a cold and a sore throat, the simplest of all remedies is hot lemon juice sweetened with honey or sugar. It is anti-inflammatory and kills germs.

Taken on an empty stomach, hot lemon juice stimulates the gallbladder and combats intestinal sluggishness.

Sweetbriar: In autumn, this wild cousin of the garden rose produces beautiful ruby-red berries.
AT LEFT

IN THE BEAUTY CABINET

To soften and whiten the hands and strengthen the nails, rub them daily with half a lemon. Also, the juice of one lemon may be added to the last rinse after shampooing, making the hair shinier and easier to comb out.

■ Red Poppies

Poppy flowers are an effective sedative and in treating insomnia are prepared either as an infusion or a syrup. Poppy is also used to stop nervous and nonproductive (dry) coughs.

Use a pinch of dried petals per cup of boiling water and let steep for a few minutes. Take this infusion right before going to bed.

Poppy flowers are soothing and anti-inflammatory for tired, irritated eyes. To make

this "lotion," prepare the petals as you would an infusion, using 2 tablespoons per quart of boiling water.

•Poppy Petal Syrup•

1 CUP DRIED PETALS

½ QUART WATER

2½ CUPS SUGAR

Let the petals steep in the boiling water overnight. Filter and add sugar. Place over low heat until the liquid becomes dark pink and has the consistency of syrup. Take 1 tablespoon at each meal (1 teaspoon per day for children).

■ Sweetbriar or Eglantine

In Germany, rose hip tea or *Hagenblüt* is a national institution. The pink infusion is as popular as common tea and is sold everywhere.

The red berries (rose hips) appear on the otherwise naked branches of the bushes in autumn. Sweetbriar often grows along country roads and forms impenetrable thickets where birds love to nest. Unfortunately for the birds, this stunning plant wasn't named for them. Its scientific name is *rosa canina,* meaning "dog rose." The name came about in antiquity, when the roots and berries were thought to cure rabies.

The flowers bloom in May and June. They are generally collected as buds, and when prepared as an infusion act as a slight laxative, as

do the leaves. The hips are picked when ripe, after the first autumn frosts, but you have to get there before the birds, as they, too, love the flaming red berries. Rose hips are mainly used for infusions but also make a delicious red-orange-colored jam.

The infusion is considered to be a stimulant, a diuretic, and a good treatment for diarrhea. It also reinforces immunity to infectious diseases. As it has a high content of vitamin C, this drink is particularly appreciated in winter, when fatigue and colds often strike.

To prepare a rose hips infusion, it is important to crush and then boil the hips for 10 minutes, using about ⅓ cup per quart of water. It is possible to blend rose hips with hibiscus flowers: The two flavors combined are a real treat.

Sweetbriar bushes are often covered with a strange reddish, hirsute growth. This is a parasite, a sort of fungus called bedegar, often used for making natural darkish-brown dyes; it is also credited with medicinal properties.

■ Lavender

The author Jean Giono came from Provence, and his descriptions of lavender made it the "soul of Haute-Provence," blanketing it in color and perfume.

"In the solitude of the Lure mountains, wild lavender grows everywhere, as far as the eye can see. At harvest-time, the evenings are lavender-embalmed. The colors of the setting sun are like litters of cut flowers. The rudimentary stills set near the tanks breathe red flames in the night; the caramel-scented smoke wafts off to enchant the dreams of those lonely souls sleeping in the desert. When you have lived these lavender nights and these days, you are forever attached to the spirit of this perfume."

Lavender flowers are gathered when they first start to bloom and should be dried on a cloth because they will fall apart. Lavender is most often used for perfuming, but it is also an excellent plant for infusions and has a most agreeable flavor.

Plant specialists recommend lavender to treat migraines, ease digestive spasms, and for certain respiratory problems. Lavender is also soothing for the nervous system.

Lavender is prepared as an infusion using

about ⅓ cup of dried flowers for 1 quart boiling water.

Lavender is also a local anesthetic. It is best used as a decoction. Apply with compresses directly on a cut, blow, bruise, or sprain. To prepare the lavender decoction, boil 3 tablespoons of flowers in 1 quart of water for 10 minutes.

For bee stings, a few flowers and leaves picked fresh and rubbed directly on the sting ease the pain and the swelling.

IN THE BEAUTY CABINET

Lavender is also extracted to obtain its essence—a few drops of lavender essence can make a normal bath a delight. The practice of using it for bathing dates to ancient Rome, where lavender was so prized that few consid-

ered bathing without it. Proof of this is found in the root of lavender's name: In Latin, *lavare* means "to wash."

To make a nice vinegar-based cleansing lotion to sweeten up bathwater and use as a hair rinse after shampooing, soak ½ cup of freshly cut flowers in 1 quart of cider vinegar. For an even more potent mixture, place the receptacle near a sunlit window for 1 or 2 weeks.

IN THE HOME

Lavender is a great pesticide. Rubbing the wood of cabinets and cupboards with essential oil keeps mites and flies away. Lavender also makes a great addition to potpourri for freshening all the rooms of the house, such as in the following recipe.

•Moist Potpourri with Rose•

This recipe requires using old roses, which are the most odiferous, but which haven't yet dried out completely. The petals should still be somewhat supple to the touch.

Amber, musk, or iris powder were once used to "fix," or preserve, fragrances. Iris powder is getting harder and harder to find and can be replaced with benzoin tincture, a resinous plant extract with an aroma akin to that of vanilla.

YOU WILL NEED:

3½ CUPS ROSE PETALS

1 TEASPOON BROKEN BAY LEAVES

1¾ CUPS LAVENDER

ZEST OF ½ ORANGE, MINCED

1 TEASPOON CINNAMON

1 TEASPOON MUSK

1 TEASPOON MACE

1 TEASPOON CLOVES

1 TEASPOON VANILLA

2 TEASPOONS IRIS POWDER OR BENZOIN TINCTURE

ROCK SALT

¼ CUP BRANDY

5 DROPS ROSE ESSENCE

In a dish or jar, blend the plants and spices in layers alternating with a layer of salt. Add the brandy and the rose essence. Mix well and let sit for at least 15 days. The dry method is much simpler because all you need to do is combine the ingredients.

■ Lemon Balm

This plant is often called citronella or bee pepper. Its rough, serrated leaves give off a strong lemon smell when crushed between the fingers. When in bloom, balm attracts swarms of bees, which is how it got its scientific name—in Greek, *melissa* means "bee." Balm makes a decorative plant for herb gardens, especially the yellow-flecked *aurea* variety. A word of caution: Like mint, balm tends to run rampant and invade other plants' territory, and so is perhaps better confined to pots.

Balm is harvested in May and June and then dried in the shade.

The leaves are used to make a delicious, sweet-tasting infusion, which is a delicious and gentle antispasmodic and facilitates digestion.

A sugar cube soaked in balm water is often recommended to women suffering from nausea in the early months of pregnancy.

A sachet of dried lavender and artemisia
freshens wardrobes and linen closets,
and keeps mites and other insects at bay.
OPPOSITE

•Balm Water•

Highly reputed for centuries, this liqueur is strong and has a powerful aroma. Long ago, it was a must in every family's medicine cabinet. Balm water was used to cure headaches, drowsiness, dizziness—and was especially recommended to women who suffered from the restrictive corsets of the day! Here is one very old recipe.

YOU WILL NEED:

½ CUP BALM LEAVES

ZEST OF ½ LEMON

1½ TABLESPOONS NUTMEG

1½ TABLESPOONS CORIANDER SEEDS

2 TEASPOONS CLOVES

2 TEASPOONS CINNAMON STICKS

1 QUART BRANDY OR 45-PROOF ALCOHOL

Soak all the ingredients together in a bottle or jar and let stand for 8 days. Next, filter and pour into a decanter or bottle.

Balm water should always be used diluted as a small spoonful in a little water, or about ten drops on a sugar cube. It should never be taken undiluted.

IN THE HOME

Balm can also be used much in the same way as vervain for a potpourri—the leaves exude sweet, lemony notes.

•Michel Guérard's Sedative Tea•

TO MAKE THE BLEND, YOU WILL NEED:

3 TABLESPOONS PASSION FLOWER

3 TABLESPOONS HAWTHORN

3 TABLESPOONS BITTER ORANGE

3 TABLESPOONS MARJORAM

3 TABLESPOONS BALM

Place the ingredients in a jar and shake to mix.

Use 2 to 3 tablespoons of this mixture per quart of boiling water.

Taken after dinner, sedative tea makes for very sweet dreams.

OPPOSITE

■ Pine and Fir Trees

The needles of pine and fir trees are heaven-sent for those who suffer from colds and respiratory infections. They should be gathered in April, when the first buds are forming and the sap is at its most concentrated. They may be dried naturally or placed in a warm oven to speed up the process.

The needles can be used to make infusions taken three times a day. Fir honey, which is dark in color and has a strong balsamic taste, is highly recommended as a sweetener for this beverage. Use about 3 tablespoons of needles per quart of water and let it steep for at least 1 hour.

Pine is also used to make essential oil: A few drops added to a hot bath clear a stuffed nose and congested lungs.

*A*n infusion of young pine shoots
is sweetened with pine honey to
create a remedy for a cough.

AT LEFT

*I*t is said that the "Queen of Hungary's Water"
allowed its namesake to conquer the heart of the
young king of Bohemia. This body splash has a
fragrance similar to that of eau de cologne.

FOLLOWING PAGES

■ Rosemary

Rosemary was called *rosmarinus* in ancient times, meaning "blue dew." There is a legend explaining that rosemary flowers are blue because the Virgin Mary dropped her coat on a rosemary bush as she fled Egypt. Ever since that day, the flowers of the plant carry the sky-blue hues of her clothing, as depicted by the artists of the time and ever since.

Rosemary is originally from the Mediterranean region and is a marvelously aromatic plant possessed of virtues known since antiquity. Easily cultivated in the garden, it can grow even in dry, poor soil. But it does need sun and space to grow, because the stems form a sort of bush that must be regularly cut back if the plant is to maintain a harmonious shape.

Rosemary can also be grown quite easily from cuttings. A fresh cutting just stuck in the ground will sprout new leaves in a few days.

Leaves and top flowers are harvested in spring and prepared as a stimulating infusion. Rosemary tea also has antispasmodic and digestive properties.

It takes only a small quantity of rosemary to make an infusion—about 1 heaping tablespoon per quart of water—and it is delicious when sweetened with rosemary honey.

A handful of rosemary leaves infused in vinegar for a few weeks makes an excellent cleansing vinegar, particularly good for softening hard water. Pour ½ cup in your bathwater, or use a few drops in your last hair rinse.

IN THE BEAUTY CABINET

During the Renaissance, rosemary was highly reputed for having kept the queen of Hungary looking young and beautiful. The queen used this "magic" elixir daily, as a body splash. The "Queen of Hungary's Water" is still held in high esteem in England, and is used as eau de toilette and cologne. Many recipes with rosemary exist, and the following is adapted from an extremely old one.

• The Queen of Hungary's Water •

You will need:

1 handful rosemary (flowers and leaves)

3 tablespoons fresh mint leaves

2 tablespoons rose petals

Zest of ½ lemon, minced

1 cup vodka, gin, or 45-proof alcohol

1 cup orange blossom water

Chop up the rosemary, mint, and rose petals.

Place all the plants and spices in a jar or earthenware pot and pour the alcohol and the orange blossom water over them.

Let mixture steep for 15 days, then filter and pour into a decanter or bottle.

The orange blossom water may be replaced with rosewater, as long as you are sure to add a little lavender (the same quantity as for the mint) or whatever other aromatic plant strikes your fancy.

• Rosemary Massage Oil •

You can also make a great massage mixture by soaking a few branches of fresh rosemary in an oil or lotion base. It relieves tired, aching muscles and smells divine. Here is a good recipe for an aromatic massage oil:

YOU WILL NEED:

1 HANDFUL FRESHLY CUT ROSEMARY

1 SPOONFUL THYME

1 SPOONFUL LAVENDER FLOWERS

A FEW MINT LEAVES

1 CUP SWEET ALMOND OR SUNFLOWER OIL

Mince the leaves and flowers and place in a bottle or a jar.

Cover in oil and allow to soak in the sun for a few weeks, stirring from time to time.

Filter and pour into bottles.

■ Sage

According to the medical scholars at Salerno, he who used sage could expect to live longer than other men, thanks to the herb's therapeutic properties. The Latin name for sage, *salvia,* means "that which saves."

Wild sage flourished and was much appreciated throughout the Mediterranean world, and it was also highly prized in Asian cultures. The Chinese were so fond of sage that they were known to exchange two cases

Blue-mauve sage flowers are lovely in bouquets or infusions.

of their best tea for a single case of sage leaves.

For teas, use either official sage (*Salvia officinalis*) or clary sage, a variety with leaves so prized among Old World herbalists that it came to be known as "tout bonne" (all good).

IN THE GARDEN

Many strains of sage may be mingled to emphasize the variety of the species' leaves and flowers—purple-leaved or golden-leaved sage looks lovely next to pineapple sage, a strain with leaves that exude a sweet scent similar to that of the pineapple fruit when crushed between the fingers.

Sage is gathered from spring to autumn. The leaves, once dried in the shade, retain their flavor for a long time. It is said that sage should not be stored in metal containers but rather in glass or even cardboard since its leaves contain an essence that causes metal to oxidize.

To prepare an infusion, use 2 to 3 tablespoons per quart of water. Sage stimulates and regulates the digestive tract. Herbalists also recommend it for women with hormonal problems. But as this is a powerful plant, it should be taken in light infusions and never to excess.

Long ago, as soon as women detected the emergence of their first dreaded gray hairs, they rinsed their hair with a strong sage infusion. This mixture was reputed to enhance brunette highlights. A rinse can be prepared with about ⅔ cup of sage per quart of water.

Dried sage leaves can also be powdered, thus creating an extraordinary, natural deodorant, which is used like talc.

IN THE KITCHEN

This delicious aromatic plant should be used generously when preparing fatty meats such as pork or cold cuts, since sage helps the body to digest cooked fat. In Italy, breaded and deep-fried sage leaves often accompany roasted or grilled meats.

In the Provence region of the south of France, there exists an aromatic bouillon that closely resembles herbal teas in its preparation. Called *aigo boulido* (literally, "boiled garlic"), it is prepared with boiling water and a few sage leaves, garlic, and olive oil. Here is the recipe.

• Aigo Boulido •

FOR EACH SERVING, YOU WILL NEED:

1 CUP WATER

2 CLOVES OF GARLIC

6 FRESH SAGE LEAVES

A FEW SPRIGS OF THYME

1 BAY LEAF

ROCK SALT

PEPPER

1 HEAPING TABLESPOON OLIVE OIL

Bring the water to a boil while peeling and crushing the garlic cloves. Place the garlic in the water, then add the sage, thyme, and bay leaf. Salt and pepper to taste.

Let simmer for about 10 minutes.

Filter the bouillon and add the olive oil just before serving.

Another, more sophisticated version of this bouillon may be made by adding a beaten egg yolk just before serving. It is often served with toast that has been rubbed with raw garlic, olive oil, and a little salt.

This soup is as flavorful as it is healthful. It favors restfulness and soothes an irritated respiratory system. Garlic is particularly recommended for poor circulation, as it thins the blood, improving its flow through the vessels.

• Sage Wine •

This wine is easy to prepare. It possesses properties that both stimulate the body and enhance the appetite.

1 QUART OF GOOD SWEET WINE OR SHERRY
(TRY A SAUMUR BLANC OR A MODEST SAUTERNES)

Steep large pieces of cut sage leaves in the wine for 10 to 15 days.

Filter the mixture and pour into a bottle or decanter.

For medicinal uses, it is both fortifying and a digestive stimulant, take one tablespoon of this preparation after meals.

Sage wine may also be served hot in wintertime, when prepared with a good Sauternes or sweet white Saumur wine:

Heat the wine and the sage leaves to a simmer and let steep for a few minutes.

Strain and serve in a thick glass, adding a sugar cube per serving.

■ Marigolds (Calendula)

You may be surprised to find that the beautiful marigold is considered a medicinal plant. Its medicinal reputation was established in the Middle Ages. The marigold's uses are mostly external: The infusion of its bright gold or yellow petals is extremely beneficial for the skin, for both cleansing and softening.

The ratio is generally about ⅓ cup of petals per quart of boiling water; the mixture is then steeped for 10 minutes. Once filtered, it is used as a gentle facial astringent after washing. This infusion will keep for several days in the refrigerator.

Taken twice a day for a week before menstruation, a marigold infusion increases the regularity of the menstrual cycle. Use about 3 tablespoons per quart of water.

When crushed and applied to warts, fresh marigold leaves help them to go away.

Although marigold petals have no scent, they retain their bright gold color when dried and make a lively addition to potpourri.

Long ago, in the Normandy region of France, marigold petals were used to color butter in winter. Milk taken from cows that were not exposed to sunlight made such a distressingly white butter that the Normans simply added marigold dye!

A marigold infusion may be used to soften the skin after cleansing.

AT LEFT

IN THE KITCHEN

Marigolds may be eaten in several different salads. The petals are delicious when sprinkled over lettuce or other tender leafy greens. The buds can also be pickled in vinegar, making an interesting sort of caper: Let the buds steep in vinegar with a branch of tarragon, a pinch of pepper, and some hot pepper if desired. It's easy.

■ Thyme

Thyme grows wild all over the Mediterranean. It has a distinctive camphorlike odor. In summer, thyme is covered with little pink flowers that bees love, and honey made from thyme is absolutely delicious. The whole of the plant is rich in essential oils: Phenol and thymol have been prized since antiquity for their stimulating, antispasmodic, and antiseptic properties.

Thyme is easy to grow in a garden or window box, on the condition that it gets enough sun. There are several interesting subspecies, such as lemon thyme and wooly thyme, a great groundcover that spreads all over the place, showing off a multitude of tiny, cinder-colored leaves. The gold-flecked leaves of the *aurea* variety bring a nice change of color to the mainly green tones found in most gardens.

Thyme leaves may be harvested and used anytime for cooking, but the flowers, used for herbal teas, are best picked when they just begin to blossom.

For infusions, use 1 to 2 tablespoons of the flowers per quart of boiling water. I prefer thyme honey as a sweetener. You can also blend thyme with other aromatics, such as marjoram, rosemary, and lemon thyme for herbal teas with a twist.

IN THE BEAUTY CABINET

To give a deep, rich shine to brown or chestnut hair, use a concentrated thyme infusion as a final rinse after shampooing.

Long ago, thyme leaves were dried and made into a powder for cleaning the teeth and disinfecting the mouth.

■ Violet

Who ever claimed that violets were modest flowers? Toward the end of March, forest floors are covered with carpets of violets, which thrive in moist, mossy ground. You have to get pretty close to the tiny five-petal blossoms in order to detect their exquisitely delicate perfume, a blend of iris and wet leaves. The Romans used to weave violets into crowns to wear at banquets. The violets were reputed to dissipate the alcohol fumes of those who had overimbibed. Plutarch wrote that "the violet and rose headpieces suppress and avoid headaches."

Violets are also recommended for sore throats and respiratory problems. In the Middle Ages, violets were used in the preparation of a syrup to treat coughs and bronchitis.

Violet infusions are made using the flowers; in fact, the stems, leaves, and roots of violets are purgative and are known to cause vomiting.

Infusions are prepared with 1 to 2 tablespoons of leaves for 1 quart boiling water.

•Colette's Violet Infusion•

The French author Colette often wrote for magazines such as *Vogue* or *Marie-Claire,* contributing recipes and advice gained in her country life at La Puisaye, where she was born. The article excerpted here was published in *Marie-Claire* during the harsh winter of 1940. It was wartime; provisions were in extremely short supply; and everyone was looking for old-fashioned recipes that were both economical and efficient:

"Pennywise housewives who gather medicinal flowers and leaves properly at the right time of the year, do you know why you find that your violet infusion is so bland? It's because you picked your violets in the sun.

They must be picked in the shade, when they first begin to bloom. Pick only the blooms without the stems and dry them in the shade, on white paper and not on a cloth. Here, we say that the cloth drinks the perfume. Also, beware of marble tables: when they are cold, the chill 'shocks' the flowers, causing them to fold up and lose part of their soul."

•Violet Cough Syrup•

All of Colette's common sense and humor have been poured into this recipe, which remains timeless in its practicality and effectiveness.

YOU WILL NEED:

½ CUP PLUS 2 TABLESPOONS VIOLET FLOWERS

1 QUART WATER

7½ CUPS SUGAR

Remove the little white part at the base of the petals and then steep them in hot water overnight.

The next day, filter the infusion and melt the sugar into it, slowly, until you get a syrupy consistency.

Take about 4 tablespoons a day for light coughs and sore throats.

121

■ The Herbal Teas of Eugénie-les-Bains

Eugénie was one of history's grandes dames, as Napoleon III 's beloved wife and empress of the French. Eugénie adored the hot springs of southwest France, and it was she who made Biarritz famous. One small village in the Landes region, particularly famous for its hot springs, was renamed in her honor, as Eugénie-les-Bains.

Almost a century later, the village of Eugénie is still famous for its springs—as well as for one of the high priests of French gastronomy, Michel Guérard. Together with his wife, Christine, Guérard has dedicated himself to converting their four houses—Eugénie's Meadows, Thrush Farm, Herb Convent, and The Pink House— into veritable havens for gourmets, particularly those who need to watch the scale.

The "parish priest's garden" makes for a beautiful promenade among a multitude of plants: Here vervain, balm, rosemary, thyme, and many other plants are used daily in teas prepared by the local herbalist.

For those wishing to slim down, Christine Guérard has composed a special blend of plants, with tasty lemon and orange accents. This drink is generally taken cold, but it is also delicious served hot. Artificial sweetener is recommended, of course.

•Christine Guérard's Slimming Tea•

This tea is a blend of plants reputed for their diuretic properties.

USE 1 TABLESPOON PER CUP

OF THE FOLLOWING MIX:

CORNSILK

COWBERRY LEAVES

HEATHER FLOWERS

CHERRY STEMS

HORSETAIL

1 CUP WATER

1 LEMON, QUARTERED

1 ORANGE, QUARTERED

1 BOUQUET FRESH MINT

Place the plants to steep in hot water, then add the quarters of half a lemon, all the orange quarters, and the mint bouquet. Filter and serve ice-cold in a carafe, adding the juice from the remaining lemon at the last minute; decorate with a few sprigs of mint.

A WORD IN CONCLUSION

*T*his book closes on a treasured child-hood memory of an old-fashioned oil lamp resting on a night table, its flame gently flickering as it warmed that night's infusion.

It was wonderful to enter this dreamworld, to venture into this room steeped in the fragrance of vervain or lime, where shadows played hide-and-seek with the tiny glow of the candle.

One day, as I was browsing in an antique shop, I happened across one of those old lamps that had once been crowned with a *tisanière*—a small-scale, potbellied teapot, which had no doubt long since been broken or lost.

I bought it and it became a little candle-holder, over which I sometimes place a bowl for infusing the tea that best suits my mood.

GENERAL INDEX

Page numbers in *italic* refer to illustrations.

RECIPE INDEX

ACKNOWLEDGMENTS

With special thanks to the following contributors:

Christine and Michel Guérard
Dina, of Liwan
Marie-Anick Lovis, of Conran
Annie, of Christian Tortu
Monsieur Pierre, of the Palais Royal herbal shop
Mariage Frères

and also . . .
Asiatides, Le Bon Marché, Caravane, la Compagnie française de l'Orient et de la Chine,
Baptiste, Denise Corbin, Despalles, Fanette, Le Bain Marie, Robert le Héros,
La Varangue, Xanadou, l'Artisan Parfumeur

Editorial Director: Laurence Basset
Layout and design: Étienne Hénocq